CONTENTS

T0014453

SUPPERTIME. 4

TWO KINDS OF
　　CARNIVORES. 6

ADAPTING TO EAT 8

AT HOME IN THE SOIL . . 10

CARNIVORE
　　CHARACTERISTICS . . . 12

SHUT YOUR TRAP! 14

PASSIVE PITCHERS. 16

UNDERWATER
　　PREDATORS 18

STICKY SUNDEWS 20

OFFENSE AS DEFENSE . . 22

GLOSSARY. 23

INDEX 24

WEBSITES. 24

SUPPERTIME

Most plants seem pretty gentle. They can't walk, talk, or fight us. Some plants have flowers that are beautiful to look at or smell. People use plants all the time—for eating, building, and more. Would it surprise you, then, to know that some plants are killers?

Carnivorous plants are plants that eat **insects** and animals. These plants use traps to catch their dinner. These traps could be in the form of a sticky liquid. Some traps work by catching animals that accidentally land on a plant. How do plants capture and **digest** their food, and why? Let's find out.

PLANT POINTER
Venus flytraps are well-known carnivorous plants. Carnivorous plants have adapted, or changed, to eat bugs and animals. They're sometimes called insectivores.

PLANT
DEFENSES

PLANTS THAT EAT

Published in 2017 by The Rosen Publishing Group, Inc.
29 East 21st Street, New York, NY 10010

First Edition

Editor: Sarah Machajewski
Book Design: Reann Nye

Photo Credits: Cover Ed Reschke/Stockbyte/Getty Images; pp. 4, 22 nico99/ Shutterstock.com; p. 5 francesco de marco/Shutterstock.com; p. 6 Cathy Keifer/ Shutterstock.com; p. 7 scaners3d/Shutterstock.com; p. 8 Sandra Caldwell/ Shutterstock.com; p. 9 Nokuro/Shutterstock.com; p. 10 joloei/Shutterstock.com; p. 11 Elliotte Rusty Harold/Shutterstock.com; p. 12 Thousandlies/Shutterstock.com; p. 13 ullstein bild/Getty Images; p. 14 Claus Meyer/Minden Pictures/Getty Images; p. 15 Panel Rey/EyeEm/Getty Images; p. 16 https://commons.wikimedia.org/wiki/ File:Rattus_baluensis_visiting_Nepenthes_rajah.png; p. 17 https://commons.wikime- dia.org/wiki/File:Nepenthes_rajah.png; p. 18 Auscape/Universal Images Group/ Getty Images; p. 19 BMJ/Shutterstock.com; p. 20 Bildagentur Zoonar GmbH/ Shutterstock.com; p. 21 Jan van Arkel/ NiS/ Minden Pictures/Getty Images.

Library of Congress Cataloging-in-Publication Data

Names: Jones, Keisha, author.
Title: Plants that eat / Keisha Jones.
Description: New York : PowerKids Press, [2017] | Series: Plant defenses
Identifiers: LCCN 2016006673 | ISBN 9781499421392 (pbk.) | ISBN 9781499421415 (library bound) | ISBN 9781499421408 (6 pack)
Subjects: LCSH: Carnivorous plants–Juvenile literature. | Plant defenses–Juvenile literature.
Classification: LCC QK917 .J66 2017 | DDC 583.75–dc23
LC record available at http://lccn.loc.gov/2016006673

Manufactured in the United States of America

CPSIA Compliance Information: Batch #BS16PK: For Further Information contact Rosen Publishing, New York, New York at 1-800-237-9932

This bug may not know it, but it will soon become dinner for this sundew.

TWO KINDS OF CARNIVORES

To date, scientists know of about 600 **species** of carnivorous plants. These plants are very different in the way they look, how they grow, and what they eat. They even trap their **prey** differently. Sometimes the only thing they have in common is that they're carnivores.

Carnivorous plants have active or passive traps. Active traps are traps that move to capture their prey. One example is a trap that closes around a bug's body. Passive traps don't move to catch prey—the prey comes to the trap. One example is a trap that a bug or animal may fall into by mistake.

VENUS FLYTRAP

A sundew wraps itself around a fly that was unlucky enough to land on its sticky leaves!

ADAPTING TO EAT

Generally, plants need sunlight, water, and food to grow. However, these things aren't always available. Sometimes a plant needs to adapt in order to survive. The ability to eat meat—such as bugs or animals—is an amazing plant **adaptation**.

Bugs and animals are the main food sources for carnivorous plants. That's where the plant gets the **nutrients** it needs to survive. This adaptation may have started long ago in plants that grew in soil that had few nutrients. The plants that could eat meat survived better than those that couldn't. Over time, the adaptation was passed on to new plants.

Carnivorous plants have found ways
to survive the special conditions in
their **environment**.

AT HOME IN THE SOIL

Carnivorous plants live in **habitats** such as bogs and fens. They're low-lying wetlands that generally get a lot of sun. The soil in these habitats is wet and high in acid. However, it's low in nitrogen, which is something most plants need to survive.

Most soils contain nitrogen in the form of something called nitrates. Plants take in nitrates through their roots. If nitrates aren't available, plants have to find nitrogen elsewhere. Bugs and animals are a great source of it. Scientists say carnivorous plants can survive on just sunlight, water, and **carbon dioxide**, but they're much healthier if they have nitrogen.

PLANT POINTER
The process of making food with sunlight, water, and carbon dioxide is called photosynthesis.

Damp habitats, such as bogs and swamps, are perfect places for carnivorous plants to grow. Not all plants can survive in these places.

CARNIVORE CHARACTERISTICS

Carnivorous plants are found all over the world, including North America! In the United States, some species are found in North Carolina and South Carolina. Other kinds of insectivores live in California and Oregon.

In general, meat-eating plants are small. Species can range from a few inches to more than 3 feet (1 m) in height. Some carnivorous plants are so small that they're hard to spot among other plants in their habitat.

Venus flytraps, pitcher plants, bladderworts, and sundews are commonly known meat eaters. Let's take a closer look at them.

PLANT POINTER
Plants that eat meat are grouped into several major families. The biggest family has about 300 species. Even the pineapple family has a few meat eaters!

This sundew's dinner is bigger than it is!

SHUT YOUR TRAP!

Venus flytraps look like something from another planet! This active insectivore is known for the spiky traps that catch prey. The traps may look like mouths, but they're actually sets of specialized leaves. A **hinge** separates the leaves, which are surrounded by spiny "teeth."

It only takes a half second for a Venus flytrap to catch its food. When a bug lands on the plant, it brushes against tiny hairs that tell the trap to snap shut. Next, the leaves give off a special liquid that breaks down the bug's body. After about 10 days of digestion, the trap opens once again.

PLANT POINTER

Some scientists say Venus flytraps can count! A trap only closes if its hairs are brushed twice within a 20-second period. Also, it only digests its prey if the hairs are brushed more than three times.

A Venus flytrap's leaves turn red from the liquid they use to digest bugs.

PASSIVE PITCHERS

Some meat-eating plants like their food to fall right into their trap. That's how pitcher plants eat. They have leaves shaped like a pitcher, which is a container for holding liquids. Some species' leaves are shaped like trumpets or jugs. The leaves form something called a pitfall trap.

The pitfall trap holds nectar that **attracts** bugs and, sometimes, animals. Drawn to the sweet smell, the prey falls inside the plant. Smooth sides or downward-pointing hairs keep the prey from crawling back out. As more food falls in, the nectar rises, and the plant begins digesting its food.

PLANT POINTER
Nepenthes rajah is the world's largest pitcher plant. It can digest rodents!

Enzymes released inside the trap digest a pitcher plant's food.

UNDERWATER PREDATORS

Bladderworts are the largest group of carnivorous plants. There are more than 200 species around the world. To find many of them, you can look underwater.

Bladderworts grow both in wet soil and in bodies of water, such as ponds, lakes, and streams. They don't have roots, but they do have specialized leaves that act as traps.

The traps are oval and have a door-like part that opens to the inside of the plant. The door gives off a sweet smell to attract prey. If the prey gets too close, it rubs the tiny hairs surrounding the door. Suddenly—snap! The door flies open, sucking the animal inside.

PLANT POINTER
Bladderworts can digest their prey in as little as 15 minutes.

Bladderworts are passive carnivores. They don't move to draw prey in. Rather, the quick flow of water through the door sucks the prey inside.

STICKY SUNDEWS

Sundews grow all over the world. These plants are named for the sticky drops of liquid on their leaves that catch the sunlight. The leaves are covered with tiny hairs that have **glands** at the tips. The hairs are also called tentacles.

The sundew's glands give off a sticky liquid that attracts insects. When an insect lands on the sundew, it gets stuck! Once the bug is caught, the tentacles wrap around its body. The plant then digests the food, which can take about four days. Once the sundew is done eating, the tentacles uncurl, and the plant waits for its next meal.

PLANT POINTER
Studies show that a sundew's tentacles wrap tighter around a bug the more it struggles to get free.

A sundew's tentacles work a lot like a spider web or flypaper. Once a bug lands on the plant, it has a hard time getting off.

OFFENSE AS DEFENSE

Carnivorous plants have one of the coolest adaptations in the plant kingdom. While this adaptation has helped these plants have a healthy diet, it's also helped them stay safe. In a way, eating meat is a defense, or something that protects the plant from predators.

Many plants give off chemicals that tell predators to stay away. This is a pretty common defense. Scientists think carnivorous plants work in the opposite way, but with the same results. The plants found a way to use the chemicals to attract bugs or animals, which they then trap and eat. Once those animals or bugs are dead, they can't hurt the plant. That's some defense!

GLOSSARY

adaptation: A change that helps an organism survive in its environment.

attract: To draw nearer.

carbon dioxide: A gas in the air that plants use to make food.

digest: To break down food inside the body so that the body can use it.

environment: The natural surroundings of a person, plant, or animal.

enzyme: A substance produced by a living organism that causes a chemical reaction.

gland: In plants, a cell or group of cells that releases substances.

habitat: The natural home of an animal or plant.

hinge: A part that connects two objects and allows them to move.

insect: A bug with six legs and one or two pairs of wings.

nutrient: Tiny substances in soil that plants need to grow.

prey: A bug or animal hunted or killed by another for food.

species: A group of living organisms that have similar traits.

INDEX

B
bladderwort, 12, 18, 19
bogs, 10, 11

C
carbon dioxide, 10

F
fens, 10

H
habitat, 10, 11, 12

N
Nepenthes rajah, 16
nitrates, 10
nitrogen, 10
nutrients, 8

P
photosynthesis, 10
pitcher plant, 12, 16, 17
predators, 22
prey, 6, 14, 16, 18, 19

S
species, 6, 12, 16, 18
sundew, 5, 7, 12, 13,
        20, 21
swamps, 11

T
tentacles, 20, 21

V
Venus flytrap, 4, 6, 12,
        14, 15

WEBSITES

Due to the changing nature of Internet links, PowerKids Press has developed an online list of websites related to the subject of this book. This site is updated regularly. Please use this link to access the list: www.powerkidslinks.com/plantd/eat